GW00503732

THE TERRIBLY PLAIN PRINCESS

PAMELA OLDFIELD

THE TERRIBLY PLAIN PRINCESS

and other stories *with pictures by*
Glenys Ambrus

HODDER & STOUGHTON
LONDON LEICESTER SYDNEY AUCKLAND

Pamela Oldfield has also written

THE ADVENTURES OF SARAH AND THEODORE BODGITT

THE WITCH IN THE SUMMERHOUSE

For Julie and Derek

ISBN 0 340 20713 2

First published in 1977
Filmset and printed Offset Litho in Great Britain for
Hodder & Stoughton Children's Books, a division of
Hodder & Stoughton Ltd, Arlen House, Salisbury Road, Leicester,
by Cox & Wyman Ltd, London, Fakenham and Reading

CONTENTS

THE TERRIBLY PLAIN PRINCESS

Once upon a time there was this terribly plain Princess. I won't beat about the bush – she was terribly plain. All the visitors at the Royal christening remarked upon it.

'How extraordinarily plain she is,' said her aunt as she handed over a solid silver spoon as a christening present.

'Quite exceptionally so,' said her cousin once removed as she put a solid gold napkin ring into the Princess's tiny hands.

I say tiny hands but her hands were a great deal larger than those of most Royal Princesses. Her mouth was wider, too, and her nose was hopelessly snubbed. She also had twenty-three freckles over her nose and cheeks.

The King and Queen watched anxiously as the pile of presents grew higher and the comments on the Princess's plainness grew franker. Finally the Lord High Chamberlain presented the child with a portrait of himself wearing his full robes of office.

'We shall be hard put to find her a husband,' he

said gloomily, shaking his head with the worry of it all. The poor Queen could bear it no longer. She burst into tears and sobbed all over the King's best ermine cloak, which did it no good.

The Princess, whose name was Sophia, lived on an island with her mother, Good Queen Matilda, and her father, Good King Ferdinand. The island was the Island of Toow and was one of a group of islands with original names like the Island of Wun and the Island of Thri. Farther over to the right was the Island of Faw but nobody talked about that one. It was uninhabited and a bit of an eyesore with trees and wild flowers all over the place and no street lighting. All the islands were surrounded by seas of an incredible blue and a golden sun shone all the time.

The terribly plain Princess thrived in this beautiful kingdom, but any hopes that she might grow out of her plainness faded with the passing of the years. She didn't look like a Princess and she didn't behave like one. Sometimes her Royal cousins from Thri and Wun would come over to visit. They would play very genteel games like 'The farmer's in his Royal den,' and 'Here we go gathering Royal nuts in May,' but the Princess Sophia was bored by it all. She would slip away to find Bert, the gardener's boy. He was her one and only true best friend in all the world – or so she told him.

Bert was also terribly plain. He had a snub nose, large hands, a wide mouth and twenty-eight freckles. He worked very hard because the gardener was bone idle and spent most of his time sleeping in a wheelbarrow in the shade of a Royal pear tree.

Bert trimmed the hedges, and weeded the paths and raked the leaves off the grass. When Bert wasn't working in the gardens he was busy with his secret plan to grow a giant blue marigold. He confided this secret to no one but the Princess Sophia – and the cook and most of his relations (and he came from a very large family).

The Princess loved to help him and together they mixed powders to sprinkle and solutions to spray. They grew a giant orange marigold and some small blue marigolds but never a giant blue one. It was very disappointing for Bert but he was a sunny sort of boy and he refused to give up hope.

When the terribly plain Princess was fifteen, Good King Ferdinand sent for the Lord High Chamberlain.

'Look here,' he said, 'what are you doing about finding a husband for the Princess Sophia?'

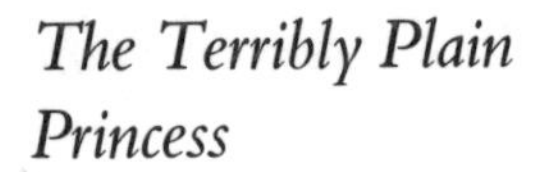

The Lord High Chamberlain bowed low.

'Everything is in hand, Your Majesty,' he said proudly, 'I think I may say in all modesty, and without fear of contradiction, though I say it myself as shouldn't —'

'Get on with it, man,' said the King. It was rather un-kingly of him but his nerves were frayed by sleepless nights spent worrying about his daughter's future.

The Lord High Chamberlain tried again. 'Bearing in mind the Princess Sophia's terrible plainness of face and largeness of hands I have now discovered the ideal husband for your daughter.'

The King sighed.

'I suppose he, too, is terribly plain,' he said.

'On the contrary, Your Majesty, Prince Archibald is of Royal and noble countenance.'

The King began to feel much happier.

'And where does this Prince live?' he asked.

'On the Island of Ayte,' said the Lord High Chamberlain.

The King lowered his voice to a whisper.

'And what is it that makes the Prince an ideal husband for the Princess Sophia?' he asked.

The Lord High Chamberlain lowered his voice also.

'Your Majesty,' he said, 'the Prince Archibald is terribly short-sighted – in a Royal sort of way. I doubt if he will notice that his bride is terribly plain.'

Good King Ferdinand was delighted. He told Good Queen Matilda who was delighted and together they told the Princess Sophia who was horrified.

'But I don't want to marry him,' she protested and she stamped her foot and looked plainer than ever. 'I want to marry Bert, the gardener's boy, and help him to grow a giant blue marigold.'

'But dearest child,' said her mother. 'The gardener's boy is terribly plain and Prince Archibald is of Royal and noble countenance.'

'Royal and noble poppycock!' said the Princess. 'I want to marry Bert.'

But her protestations went unheeded and the date was set for the wedding. You may well be wondering what Bert had to say about all this. The fact is that he didn't say anything because he had designed a square parasol to shelter the marigolds from the sun's rays at mid-day and was trying to decide the best position for it.

On the Island of Ayte, Prince Archibald was not looking forward to his coming betrothal, either, because he was a confirmed bookworm. His rooms in the palace had books where books should be and books where books shouldn't be. Scattered among the books were various pairs of spectacles to help him with his reading. (There were times when his parents worried about him.)

The day of the Royal wedding dawned bright and clear. The Royal party set sail from the Island of Ayte in the Good Ship Aytee, bound for the Island of Toow.

The Princess Sophia waited on the quayside with Good King Ferdinand and Good Queen Matilda and the Lord High Chamberlain and hundreds of lesser mortals. The terribly plain Princess wore a beautiful gown of white and gold lace and a rather thick veil. As the Prince's ship drew alongside the quay a great cheer went up from the Princess's supporters and the Prince put down his book and went up on deck. It was a proud moment for the people of Toow when the Prince Archibald, of Royal and noble countenance, prepared to meet the terribly plain Princess Sophia.

But it was not to be. It so happened that the Prince Archibald had forgotten to take off his reading spectacles and put on his walking-about spectacles. Instead of stepping on to the ship's gangplank he missed it by a good few inches and stepped straight into the incredibly blue sea!

Now, although the people of Toow were nice, well-mannered people, it isn't every day you can see a Royal Prince plopping into the water like that. I have to admit that they all fell about laughing. Some of them laughed so much that *they* fell into the water as well.

Poor Prince Archibald was very upset. As soon as he was fished out of the water he gave orders to sail back to Ayte and turned to the next chapter in his book. The terribly plain Princess Sophia was also upset. She ran away to find Bert and weep on his

shoulder, but when she did find him he was at the top of a step-ladder, adjusting the square parasol over his precious marigold plants. The Princess fell to her knees on the grass below him, and wept terribly plain tears all over the marigold.

When Bert came down five minutes later to see what was going on he could hardly believe his eyes. The marigolds were beginning to grow! The plants grew taller and taller and produced giant buds which burst into bloom. Yes! You've guessed it. Bright blue marigolds!

That's almost the end of the story. Bert was awarded a medal – the Gardener's Silver Cross – and he was allowed to marry the Princess. They went to live on the Island of Faw where they raised many new and wonderful plants with the help of Princess Sophia's terribly plain tears. (She could cry to order by thinking how nearly she had married Prince Archibald!) Oh yes! They also raised a large family of happy, but terribly plain, children!

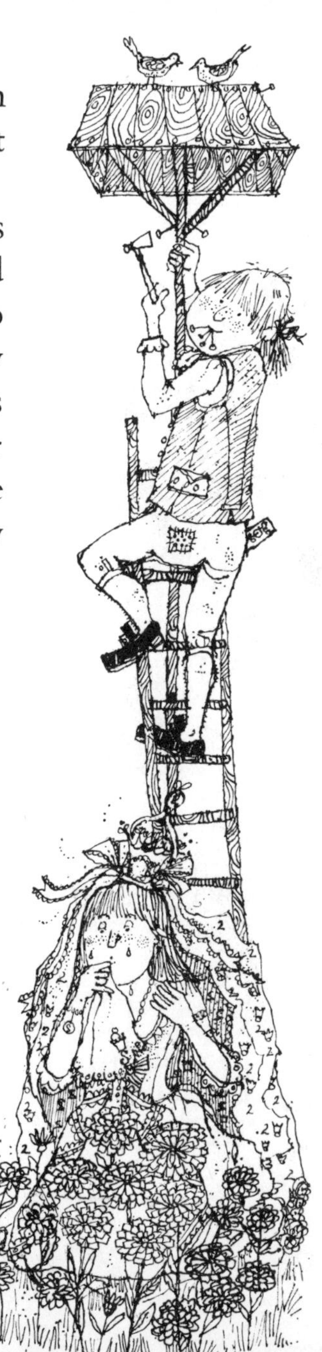

THE UNWANTED GIANT

One day a giant moved into a cave just outside the little town of Caspur. To everyone's dismay he seemed to be settling in for a long stay. Now some giants can be an asset. They are very strong and can do helpful things, such as lifting away trees that have been blown down on to the road, or holding up bridges that are about to collapse. Unfortunately, however, this giant, whose name was Bop, was the other kind of giant. He was a liability. That means he did unhelpful things such as knocking down houses and treading all over fields of barley with his big feet. So, of course, nobody liked Bop, and they wanted to get rid of him.

'He snores so loudly, too,' said one of the men.

'The noise is like the rumble of thunder and wakes up my children, night after night.'

'And he's so dirty,' said one of the ladies, wrinkling up her nose at the very thought of it. 'He never washes, and he never combs his hair – and I've heard that his cave is a disgrace! We don't want him here.'

'And his clothes!' said another lady. 'That terrible old animal skin he wears is almost threadbare. And the songs he sings! They are not at all respectable. He is giving the town a bad name. We must send him away at once.'

So a petition was prepared. At the top of a long, long sheet of paper they wrote the following words:

> '*The people of the town of Caspur wish to make it known that the giant Bop is no longer welcome to stay, and should remove himself forthwith and as quickly as possible.*'

Then everyone in the town signed it and the list of names reached all the way to the bottom of the paper. It all took a very long time. While Bop was asleep they crept up to his cave and left the petition outside, weighted down with a large stone so that it shouldn't blow away.

Bop woke up next morning and was pleased to find so much paper handy. He screwed it up into little twists and lit his fire with it to heat the milk for his early morning cocoa.

'Right then,' said the Mayor crossly. 'We will have

to picket his cave, day and night. We'll have a rota.'

It was beginning to get quite exciting. The young men painted huge banners saying GIANT, GO HOME and they took turns, ten at a time, to march up and down outside Bop's cave. Sometimes, for a change, they sang 'Why are we waiting' and shook rattles and banged saucepans.

Bop was very interested by it all. He couldn't read so he didn't know what the banners were about. He didn't know why they were waiting, so he couldn't tell them, but he was flattered by their attention and began to feel really at home, which wasn't the idea at all. His snores grew louder and his songs less respectable and still he didn't wash or comb his hair. The townspeople were beginning to feel decidedly gloomy about the whole business.

'Right then,' said the Mayor again. 'We will have to send in the army.' Someone reminded him that they didn't have an army.

'Then we'll get one,' he said, and they began at once. Twenty brave men and true were recruited and training began.

The men learned how to salute, and how to polish their boots. They dug a great many trenches and every morning they folded their sheets and blankets into

neat squares. They learned a very jolly marching song and went home on leave and came back again. They did everything that an army is supposed to do, but before they learned how to fight, Bop slipped on the mountain one day and broke his leg.

It took seventeen pounds of plaster of Paris and half a mile of bandage to set the broken bone and, of course, he had to stay in hospital. (They had to empty one of the wards to make room for him and he had to sleep on the floor.) But he was very brave about it and the people began to feel sorry for him. The nurses washed him and combed his hair. Some of the ladies in the town made him a pair of giant trousers and a giant shirt. Even more ladies set to and cleaned up his cave. They threw out all the rubbish, swept it clean, washed up the pots and pans and put fresh flowers on the flat rock that Bop used for a table.

Not to be outdone the men dug over a piece of ground outside the cave and turned it into a garden. They planted neat rows of lettuce and beetroot and at the entrance to the cave they planted a large pink rambler rose.

When at last Bop came out of hospital, in his new shirt and trousers, and saw his cave he was quite overcome. Everyone cheered and there was a lot of merrymaking. The townspeople went to bed that night happy that Bop was now a respectable citizen and that all their worries were over.

But left to himself, Bop began to have terrible doubts. His cave looked so empty without all the rubbish, and the new shirt and trousers felt stiff and uncomfortable. He tried to sing one of his favourite songs but it didn't sound right. So he took off his new clothes and put on his comfortable old animal skin. Then he mussed up his hair and tiptoed quietly out of the cave, through the town, and away.

When the townspeople woke up next morning they were dismayed to find that their unwanted giant had finally gone.

THE SILVER KEY

Ben was a simple lad and he led a simple life. Each morning he rose with the dawn and took his father's sheep up into the mountains to find good grass. At mid-day he ate a simple meal – a lump of cheese and an apple – and he washed it down with water from a spring nearby. Each evening he took his father's sheep down the mountain and after supper he went to bed. So you can see he had plenty of time to think and he pondered such matters as whether to eat the cheese or the apple first and how many beans make five.

One morning as he was making his way up the mountain path he met a man sitting outside a cave. He was poorly dressed and had an air of great sadness. Ben smiled at him and said 'Good morning', hoping for a little conversation to brighten his day, for it was rare that he met anyone on the mountain and he was curious.

'Good morning,' said the man and his air of sadness deepened visibly.

'You look very unhappy,' said Ben. 'Is there any way I can help you?'

'Maybe there is and maybe there isn't,' said the man, 'for you look like a bright lad and I am in great trouble. It's like this. I am not really a poor man but a royal prince but all my treasure has been stolen by a wicked goblin and is hidden in a cave deep underground. Without the royal treasure I cannot reclaim my throne. I am indeed an unhappy man.'

Ben was thrilled by this story but he was puzzled, too.

'Why do you not go down into the cave,' he asked, 'and find your treasure? Why do you need the help of a bright lad like me?'

The man sighed deeply.

'Would you believe that I am allergic to underground caves?' he said. 'As soon as I go into an underground cave I come out in a terrible rash of bright blue spots, and start to sneeze. I have been to the best doctors in the land but no one can help me. Will you go down into the cave for me and find my treasure? You will be well rewarded, I promise you.'

Ben felt very flattered that the prince needed his help and willingly agreed to go down into the cave. The prince said he would look after the sheep and the cheese and apple until Ben returned.

'Will the wicked goblin be down in the cave?' said Ben nervously. 'I have never met one before.'

The prince handed him a small silver key.

'Take this,' he said. 'It is a magic key and will keep you safe from all harm.'

Ben took the key and stepped into the cave. It was very gloomy but he could just see a tunnel at the far end of the cave and he set off bravely along it, the silver key held tightly in his hand.

Now I regret to have to tell you that the prince was not a prince at all, but a wily rogue. The silver key was not a magic key, either. The wily rogue had found it that very morning lying on the pathway and had no idea to which lock it belonged. As soon as Ben had gone he ate the cheese and then the apple and then hurried off towards the far hills, taking all the sheep with him!

Meanwhile poor Ben was having a terrible time. The tunnel was long and dark and sloped steeply downwards. It twisted and turned and Ben expected to meet the wicked goblin at every corner. At last he sat down to rest and think.

'If I weren't such a bright lad I would give up,' he told himself, 'but the prince is depending on me and I must go on until I have found the treasure.'

So saying he continued his difficult and dangerous journey until one hour and eleven minutes later he came to a tiny door cut in the rock at the end of the tunnel. There was no handle on the door but a tiny keyhole and Ben found that the silver key fitted perfectly. He turned it and the rock door swung open. The door was so small that Ben was only just able to squeeze through. He found himself in a room that was bare except for a table and three hundred and sixty-two cobwebs. On the table was a silver key, slightly larger than the previous one. The key opened another slightly larger door which led into a slightly larger room. This, too, was bare except for a table and four hundred and thirty-three cobwebs. On the table was a key. Need I tell you it was slightly larger than the previous one?

Ben sat down on the edge of the table to rest and think.

'If I weren't such a bright lad I would give up,' he told himself, 'but it seems to me I have a choice. I can go back. I can go on. Or I can sit here and starve to death.'

He thought very deeply for a very long time and then decided to go on. It was a good thing he did for the very next room was not at all bare. It had a table, a key, five hundred and seventy-one cobwebs and a large bird's nest. In the nest was a large glossy black egg. There was no treasure. Ben picked up the egg and tucked it under his arm. Opening the next door he was surprised to find himself back on the pathway and even more surprised to find no sign of the prince or his sheep, not to mention the cheese and the apple.

He went home and told his father everything that had happened. His father was not at all pleased to learn that Ben had lost the sheep and had spent all day underground with nothing to show for his efforts but a glossy black egg.

'You are a foolish ninny!' he roared, boxing Ben soundly on the ears. 'You have been tricked by a wily rogue.'

Ben tried to think but it isn't easy when you are being boxed on the ears. Before he could reach any conclusion there was a cracking from the glossy

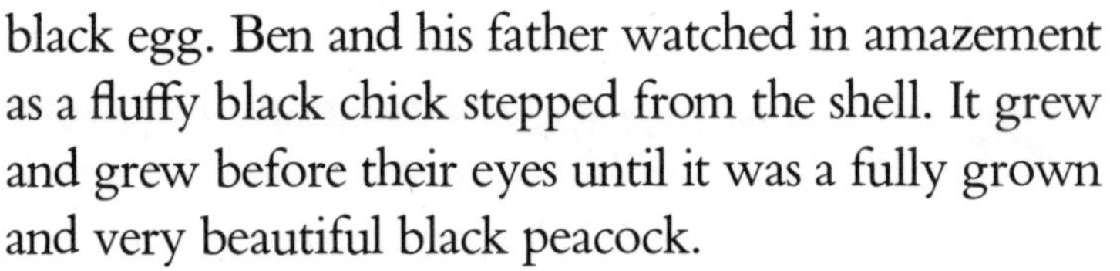

black egg. Ben and his father watched in amazement as a fluffy black chick stepped from the shell. It grew and grew before their eyes until it was a fully grown and very beautiful black peacock.

'A black peacock!' whispered Ben's father. 'That is the rarest bird in the world. The King will pay a handsome price for such a bird. Benjamin, my son, you are a bright lad and no mistake. I have always said so.'

Ben was pleased to hear him say so and even more pleased that he was no longer being boxed on the ears. They gave the black peacock some scraps of bread and a drink of water. It was an amiable creature

and settled down for the night on a pile of hay. Next morning they sent word to the King and he dashed round with a bag of gold and took the black peacock back to the palace where it lived a life of great luxury.

There was enough gold to buy another flock of sheep and Ben resumed his simple life, and was well satisfied. He found it very pleasant to be a bright lad with time to ponder such matters as whether to eat the cheese or the apple first and how many beans make five . . .

THE CHANCELLOR WHO WOULDN'T SMILE

Once upon a time there lived a Lord High Chancellor. He lived all by himself (except for the servants) in a large, draughty castle and he never went out and no one ever came in. This was because he was such a bad-tempered, ill-mannered, unreasonable man that no one liked him. Whenever anyone had to speak to him they made it as brief as possible. Even the King didn't like him and never went to the castle, preferring to telephone or write letters.

Now the Lord High Chancellor didn't know he was bad-tempered, ill-mannered and unreasonable and he couldn't understand why he had no friends.

'I live among unfriendly people,' he wrote in his diary. 'I will live and die in this lonely castle and no one will care.' Which is rather sad.

One day a scullery maid came to work in the castle. She was a happy soul, always laughing and singing and she had so many friends she had lost count of them all. Unfortunately she was also a rather clumsy girl and very forgetful. She dropped loud objects like tin trays and buckets and she broke fragile

objects like cups and saucers. She was always forgetting what work she had done and doing it again and not doing some work she ought to have done. She was often shouted at for her clumsy and forgetful ways and that made the Lord High Chancellor even more bad tempered than usual and at last he sent for the cook.

'How am I supposed to do my very important work with all this noise going on?' he demanded angrily. 'I cannot think straight. Bangings and crashings and shouting and singing! The hall has been scrubbed three times today and my favourite teapot has lost its spout. This castle is becoming a bear garden!'

The poor cook didn't know what a bear garden was but the look on the Lord High Chancellor's face frightened her half to death. She promised to speak very severely to the scullery maid, and sent for her right away.

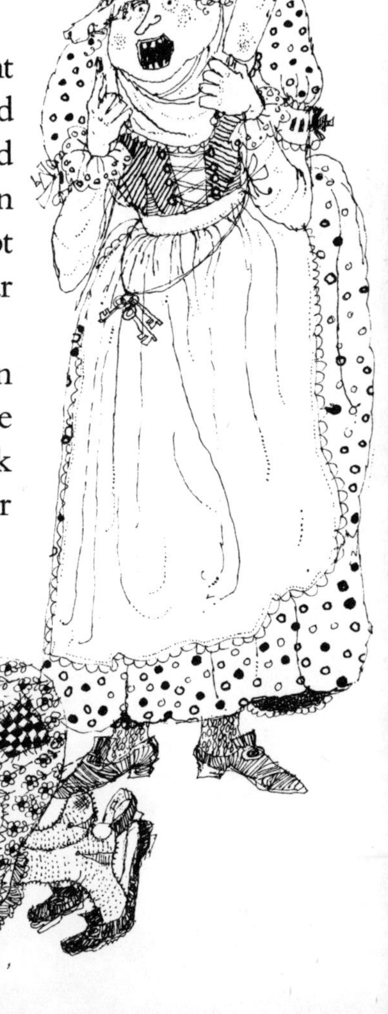

'This castle is becoming a bear garden,' she told the scullery maid. 'You must stop all this noise and think about what you are doing or it will be the sack for you, my girl.'

The scullery maid tried to look very sorry but there was a twinkle in her eye because the cook's cap was crooked and she looked rather funny.

'Now hurry up and finish scrubbing the dining-room,' said the cook. The poor girl burst out laughing because she wasn't scrubbing the dining-room at all – she was scrubbing the hall for the fourth time that day! She laughed and laughed and the cook shouted at her to stop and her cap slipped right down over her eyes. The scullery maid laughed louder than ever.

'That settles it,' roared the cook. 'Out you go, my girl, and don't you show your face here again.'

The poor scullery maid was quite hysterical by this time. Tears of laughter were rolling down her face. When the gardener came in to see what the commotion was all about he thought she was really crying and begged the cook to give her another chance. The cook boxed his ears for his impudence and the scullery maid laughed so much she got a stitch and had to sit down on a handy stool.

Suddenly the Lord High Chancellor appeared in the doorway. He looked more bad-tempered, ill-mannered and unreasonable than ever before in his life. The scullery maid stopped laughing and wiped her eyes on a corner of her apron. The gardener slipped out of the kitchen and hid himself in the potting shed. The cook ran weeping to her bedroom, she was so upset, and the Lord High Chancellor stood glaring down at the scullery maid. She looked a sorry sight in her ragged clothes and he was surprised to find himself feeling sorry for her.

After a long silence he gave a little cough and said, 'Er . . . there, there . . . er . . . my dear . . .' He wasn't used to saying nice things to people and he wasn't quite sure how to go about it. 'Um . . . er . . . don't cry now . . . um . . .'

He looked so awkward that the scullery maid was afraid she was going to laugh again and that would never do. She clapped a hand over her mouth and ran past the Lord High Chancellor, down the castle steps and out into the dark wood. She ran and ran and ran.

After she had gone peace descended on the castle. The Lord High Chancellor finished writing an important letter. The cook made an apple pie. The

gardener dug over the rosebed. It was very quiet. It was quiet the next day and the day after that. It was very quiet for a long time.

The Lord High Chancellor wrote lots of important letters and the King telephoned once or twice – I think it was twice. The Lord High Chancellor wrote in his diary, 'I live among unfriendly, quiet people. I will live and die here and no one will care . . . and the hall needs a good scrub.'

When he could bear it no longer he sent for the cook.

'Find the scullery maid,' he said 'and tell her to be my scullery maid again. I miss her laughter and singing. I even miss hearing her drop things. She must come back.'

Well, they found the scullery maid after a long search but she had gone up in the world. She was no longer a scullery maid but a parlour maid with every other Saturday off. She did not want to go back to scrubbing floors and no one could blame her. So the Lord High Chancellor asked her to marry him. She had to say 'Yes' because he looked so awkward when he said nice things to people, and they were married the very next week.

Now if you think that being married to a happy wife changed the Lord High Chancellor you are wrong. He was still bad-tempered, ill-mannered and unreasonable – but in a happy sort of way!

THE LONELY MERMAID

Merlini was a mermaid. She had a silver fish tail and long silver curls, bright sea-green eyes and long silver eyelashes. She was more beautiful than any other mermaid – but she hated the water. She spent all day sitting on a rock in the sunshine while her friends dived and swam in the cool green sea. She was, of course, very lonely and her family spent many anxious hours worrying about her.

'She'll grow out of it, I expect,' said her father hopefully, when she was still only a merbaby, but he was wrong.

'She will get bored on that rock, all by herself,' said her aunt, when she was a little older, 'and she will want to join her friends.' But she was wrong, too.

'She's just being stubborn,' said grandmother. 'She needs a good "talking-to".' But the 'talking-to' did not do any good, either, and finally her parents took her to a merdoctor. He examined her carefully and shook his head.

'It is a very rare case,' he said, 'but your daughter simply does not know how to swim. You will have to teach her.'

So they bought Merlini a red swimming cap with flowers all over it and a rubber ring and tried to coax

her into the shallow water for a swimming lesson. But as soon as she found herself in the water she began to scream and splash about, and scrambled back on to the rock as fast as she could. There she sat, in the red swimming cap and rubber ring, weeping bitterly.

The family began to despair.

'Do you think she would swim if her life depended on it?' suggested her uncle. 'Suppose we pull her into deep water. It does sound drastic but we may have to be cruel to be kind. She is growing up and who will want a merwife who sits on a rock all day?'

Reluctantly they agreed to try it. One day while Merlini was sunbathing on the rock they reached up and pulled her suddenly into the deep water. Poor Merlini! It was almost the end of her. She sank like a stone, down and down and had to be rescued. At last her family gave up. Merlini, their beautiful merdaughter, would never know the joys of life beneath the waves.

'She will waste her life on that lonely rock,' said her mother, 'and it is my greatest sorrow, but what else is to be done?' What else indeed?

They left Merlini to her lonely life and the days passed, and more days. Merlini sat in the sunshine and combed her beautiful silver curls. Sometimes she sang to herself and sometimes she talked to the sea birds who settled on the rock to rest. She often wore the red swimming cap with flowers all over it and it was this bright colour that caught the eye of a fisherman one day. He was curious to know what it was and rowed nearer. Imagine his surprise when he saw Merlini, sitting on the rock, a few silver curls showing beneath the red cap. The mermaid was just as surprised as he was and stared at the young man speechlessly. He did not speak a word for fear of frightening her away but sat in the boat and watched her. Silently he rowed away again but returned the next day.

He came day after day, never speaking, but soon he grew bolder and would sit beside her on the rock. Sometimes he brought scraps of bread and together they fed the birds. Merlini had never been so happy, but her family and friends watched them anxiously from beneath the waves.

The lonely mermaid fell in love with the silent fisherman. She longed each day for the sight of his boat, and then dreaded the moment when he rowed away and left her alone. Of the young man's feelings she had no idea, for still he did not speak. One day she could bear it no longer. As the boat dwindled in

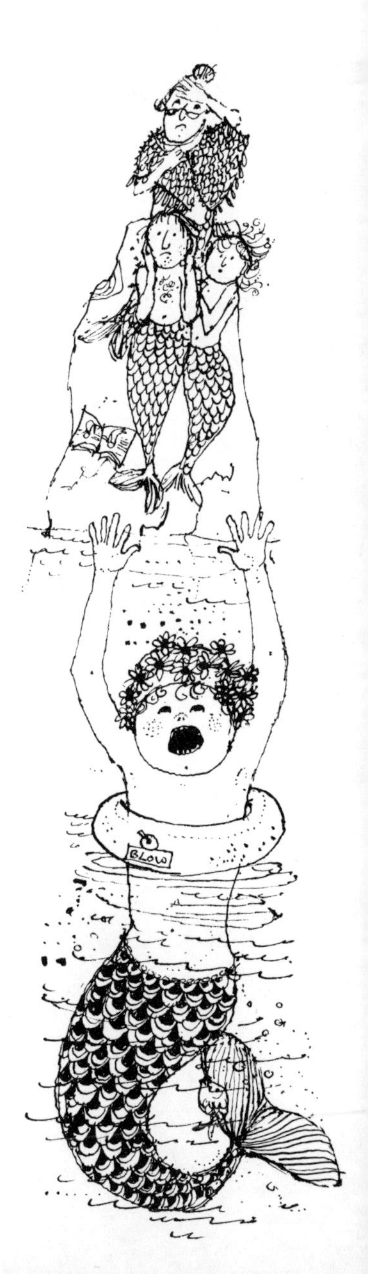

the distance she gave a little cry, dived into the water and swam after him. Yes, she swam! Her family and friends watched in amazement as she skimmed through the waves, her long silver hair streaming behind her.

'Wait for me! Wait for me,' she cried, but he could not hear her and rowed steadily on. By the time she reached the shore he had pulled the boat up on to the beach and was walking away across the sand.

Then a sad thing happened. Before Merlini could call to him again a girl came running towards the young man and greeted him with a kiss. They walked away together hand in hand and Merlini was left at the water's edge, alone. Sadly she pulled off the little red cap and dropped it on to the sand. Turning, she dived back into the water and swam out to sea.

The young man found the red cap next day and puzzled over it. He rowed out to the rock day after day for many weeks, but never saw the mermaid again. Slowly, she was learning the joys of a new life beneath the waves, and she was never lonely again.

VIOLA AND THE OGRE

I expect you've noticed how in fairy tales brave young men are always rescuing damsels from terrible danger. It's just one of those things and it seems to work out very well unless, of course, there's a shortage of

terrible danger and that is what happens in this story.

Once upon a time there was a kingdom that was so peaceful and untroubled there was no need for damsels to be rescued from anything and it was dreadfully boring for them. They began to grumble among themselves, and then the brave young men began to grumble, and the grumbling came at last to the ears of the King. Now he was a good man and

he wanted everyone to be happy, so he declared the second week in July 'Save-a-Damsel Week'.

'But my dear,' said the Queen gently, 'how can anyone save-a-damsel if there is nothing to save her from?'

The King sighed. She was right. (She was always right!)

'I have thought of that,' he told her, 'and' (here he had a sudden flash of inspiration) 'I shall advertise.'

He then ordered the Royal Artist to design some eye-catching posters and he sent them to all the neighbouring kingdoms inviting any dragons and/or ogres to settle in the area. The result was very disappointing. The two dragons who turned up were so young and foolish that the King had to give them their return fare and sent them home again. The only ogre was a sort of drop-out who didn't believe in violence and only wanted to be left alone (and anyway he was a vegetarian). The King gave him a nice cave and they left him alone. So he was no good.

Save-a-Damsel Week arrived and still there was no danger. Tuesday came and went and so did Wednesday. It was a truly dreadful state of affairs. Now a certain young man named Tomas loved a certain young girl named Viola who loved him in return.

This was very convenient except that Viola's father was opposed to their marriage because Tomas had sticking-out ears. Viola's father didn't care for the idea of a brood of grandchildren with sticking-out ears. It was rather unreasonable of him, I admit, but we can't all be perfect and the fact remains that he did hope that Viola would eventually meet and marry someone else. But Tomas was a nice, bright, likeable lad and he felt sure he would win the approval of Viola's father if he could rescue Viola from terrible danger. When 'Save-a-Damsel Week' arrived he rushed about in search of some but, as I've already explained, the danger simply did not materialise.

If you are now feeling sorry for Tomas, you needn't be. Between his sticking-out ears he had a good brain and he often used it. On this occasion he decided to disguise himself as an ogre and carry Viola off into the forest. He would then nip home, remove the disguise, and go back to rescue her. It was a neat plan, and the first part worked very well. He made himself a wild-looking wig by unravelling some rope and bought himself a large joke nose and some protruding teeth. He cut a hole in an old fur rug and pulled it over his head to make a quite presentable tunic. A club was easily achieved by knocking some

nails through a chunky piece of tree root, and he finished the job by smearing himself with mud. The final effect was so awful that when he looked at himself in the mirror it gave him a nasty fright and he had to sit down for a few minutes to recover before carrying out the next part of his plan.

He waited until it was dark and then crept into Viola's garden and hid behind some rhododendrons. Next morning when Viola came out of her cottage to go to the market he leapt out on her, roaring ferociously, and dragged her along the village street towards the forest. Her frightened screams roused the entire village and everyone crowded the street to watch in delighted horror. Fortunately for Tomas no one raised a finger to help her because all the other brave young men had grown tired of waiting for someone to rescue and had gone fishing. (In fact Viola wasn't really frightened at all because she had recognised Tomas's sticking-out ears and was thoroughly enjoying the drama of it.) She carried right on screaming and Tomas carried right on roaring although he was getting a bit hoarse by this time.

Just as it seemed his plan had succeeded an unexpected snag arose. They suddenly met the real ogre! He was on his way to market with a string bag to beg a few vegetables for his dinner. It is difficult to say which of the three was more surprised. Viola and Tomas were very confused but the poor non-violent vegetarian drop-out ogre was terrified. He trembled so much that the string bag fell from his fingers. But for all his peaceful ways he was no coward and, seeing a damsel in such terrible danger, he felt obliged to try and rescue her. He threw himself upon Tomas and bowled him over.

Poor Viola began to scream in earnest because she did not want Tomas to be killed, but Tomas did not make any sound at all because he was too busy wrestling with the ogre. They rolled backwards and forwards on the dusty ground with a great many grunts and groans, until at last Tomas's joke nose fell off. When the real ogre saw that he was not an

ogre the expression on his face was so funny that Tomas burst out laughing and took off the wig and the protruding teeth. After a moment the real ogre saw the funny side of it too and they laughed and laughed until the tears ran down their grimy faces. They slapped each other on the back so heartily that they both got hiccups and that made them laugh even

more until they grew quite hysterical and rolled helplessly about on the grass, glad to be alive and out of danger.

When they finally looked for Viola she was nowhere to be seen. She had been rescued by a very nice-looking man with flat ears (he had given up fishing having lost his bait) who was at that very moment asking Viola's father for her hand in marriage and getting it. After the initial shock Tomas discovered that he did not mind all that much and he and the ogre became firm friends. Tomas spent many a happy hour in the ogre's cave learning about vegetarian cooking, and the ogre often visited Tomas's home where they played chess together well into the night.

It's incredible, really, how well it all worked out in the end.

ROSAMARA

Once upon a time there was a farmer who had a daughter whose name was Rosamara. She was a very beautiful but very wilful girl and her father was in despair over her.

'That girl of mine will never do as she is told,' he

wailed. 'One of these days she will come to some harm and it will be no one's fault but her own!'

He was right, of course. Fathers often are. This is how it happened. One evening he sent her into the forest to gather wood for the fire. He told her for the umpteenth time not to stray from the path. Well, as soon as she was out of sight of the house she decided she would rather gather bluebells than firewood and skipped off among the trees.

Unfortunately for her she skipped a bit too far and by the time night fell she had lost the path altogether and was quite definitely lost. We all know it was her own fault, but that did not make it any easier to bear. The forest was full of shadows and strange noises. She was so lonely and frightened that she sat down under a tree and began to weep. It wasn't very practical but it was the only thing she could think of.

Suddenly an old man appeared. He had a kind face and held out his arms to her.

'Are you lost, my dear?' he said kindly. 'Come with me and I will give you shelter until the morning.'

Rosamara didn't know that he was a powerful wizard in disguise and she ran to him and took his hand. The moment she did so her legs grew weak and would not support her and her voice grew faint so

that she could not cry out. The old man changed into a wizard before her very eyes and dragged her away to his home in the deepest part of the forest. His home was a tall thin tower that reached up into the clouds like a giant reed.

There she became his servant, working from sunrise to sunrest with little food and many a harsh word, and her life was wretched indeed. And so it might have remained but for her anxious father who had half the village out searching for news of her. After many weeks a woodcutter reported that he had heard sounds of weeping at the topmost window of the wizard's tower. At these words a great dismay fell upon them all. The wizard was well known for his evil ways and there seemed little hope of rescue for the unfortunate Rosamara.

But I have told you that Rosamara was beautiful as well as wilful and there were many young men in the village who wished to win her hand. One of these was the dreamy son of the local miller. He had golden hair and blue eyes and he spent most of his days composing poetry to Rosamara's beauty, but he was too shy to tell her of his devotion so she was quite unaware of it. Now as soon as the dreamy young lad heard of her whereabouts he decided he must be near her in her hour of need. He took a large basket of peaches (which were his favourite fruit) and a pencil and notebook and settled himself down at the foot of the wizard's tower to compose some more poems to his beloved. The wicked wizard looked down on him in amazement.

'That dreamy young man is either very brave or very foolish and I'm inclined to think the latter! He is of no consequence.' And he turned his attention to the many other young lads who were trying to rescue Rosamara.

He gave them full marks for effort. One tried to reach her with a long, long ladder, but just as he drew level with the windowsill the wizard, with a wink of his eye, turned the ladder into rubber and it bent over and threw the poor lad into a very prickly briar. Another dug a tunnel beneath the wall, but the wizard, with a snap of his fingers, diverted it northwards and he is tunnelling still for all I know. The

blacksmith's son dared to challenge the wizard to a duel but he was turned into a frog for his impudence. (He turned back into the blacksmith's son after a week but his voice was never quite the same again. It sounded a bit croaky – and he suddenly lost interest in Rosamara and married someone else.)

Now while all these exciting things were happening, the miller's son still sat at the foot of the tower, scribbling away and eating peaches. It so happened that one of the peach stones which he threw down was magic and started to grow. It put down roots and then it sent up a small shoot. Nobody noticed it at all. The miller's son was too busy writing, although he did think it was getting a bit on the shady side as the little plant grew higher and higher. Rosamara was too busy working. When she wasn't working she was crying at the top of the tower and it didn't leave her much free time for noticing things.

So the magic peach tree grew higher and higher until at last the topmost branch was level with Rosamara's window. One day she stopped crying for a moment to look for a clean handkerchief, and noticed the tree outside her window. Her joy knew no bounds. Without a backward glance she climbed out of the window and down through the branches of

the peach tree. Away she ran, back to her father's farm where I'm pleased to say she wasn't wilful again for three whole weeks!

The miller's dreamy son didn't even know she had gone, but the wizard did. When he saw the peach tree he flew into a terrible rage. With a nod of his head he turned the dreamy young lad into a beautiful downy peach.

THE WICKED WOOD GOBLIN

Once upon a time there was a wood. It was a pleasant place with sunlight shining through the trees and bluebells growing among the ferns. The village folk took a short cut through the wood when they went to the market in the next town and the children liked to picnic there and gather bluebells.

One day a wicked goblin moved into the wood, and I'm afraid he changed everything. He put a spell

on the wood, making it dark and cold. No flowers grew and no birds sang. He encouraged large black rats to live among the tree roots and he filled the branches with owls and bats, and put snakes and spiders in the grass. If anyone dared to walk through the wood he would jump out and frighten them half to death for he was ugly as well as wicked, with small red eyes, a big nose and horrible crooked teeth.

So naturally the village folk had to go the long way round when they went to the market and they were pretty fed up with the wicked goblin.

Now there were three brothers living in the village and they went to market every day to sell vegetables

MARKET
10 MILES

and fruit from their garden. They soon grew tired of walking the long way round and decided to try and put an end to the wicked goblin.

One morning the youngest brother began to walk along the path through the wood. He whistled loudly as he walked so that the goblin would hear him. Sure enough the goblin leaped out from behind a bush.

'Who dares to . . .' He stopped in surprise and looked at the youngest brother in amazement. The youngest brother was wearing an ENORMOUS hat. It came well down over his ears and eyes and the young man could hardly see out from under it. The hat was very high and the brim was very wide.

'Why are you wearing that ridiculous hat?' asked the goblin, forgetting to roar and shout.

'I'm wearing it to protect my head,' said the youngest brother. 'I am terrified of bats and I'm afraid one may fly down and tangle its claws in my hair.'

The wicked goblin immediately turned himself into a very large bat and flew at the young man's hat, beating with his wings and scrabbling with his claws and trying to knock it off. The poor young man took to his heels and ran until he reached the other side of the wood where he was safe.

'My middle brother will be coming through your wood tomorrow,' he shouted defiantly. 'He's *very* brave and you won't frighten *him*!'

The next morning the middle brother started to walk through the wood. He, too, whistled loudly and the goblin dropped out of the branches of a tree and began to shout.

'Who dares to walk through . . .' He stopped suddenly and stared. The middle brother was wearing an ENORMOUS coat. The sleeves were so long they covered his hands and the coat reached down to his ankles. The coat was of thick material and it was buttoned right up to the neck.

'Why are you wearing that ridiculous coat?' asked the goblin, really wanting to know.

'I am wearing it to protect my body,' said the middle brother. 'I am terrified of wolves, but if I meet one it will not bite me through this thick coat.'

The wicked goblin immediately turned himself into a wolf and sprang at the young man. He tried to bite him through the cloth but it was too thick. The young man took to his heels and ran until he came to the other side of the wood where he was safe.

'My eldest brother will be coming through your wood tomorrow,' he shouted defiantly.

'He's *very* brave and you won't frighten *him*!'

The next morning the eldest brother started to walk through the wood. He sang loudly and out of tune and the goblin came rushing out from beneath a bramble.

'Who dares to walk through my . . .' He could hardly believe his eyes. The eldest brother was wearing a pair of ENORMOUS boots. They were made of black leather and came well up past his knees. True, they were highly polished and the buckles gleamed, but they were about ten sizes too big!

'Why are you wearing those ridiculous boots?' asked the goblin, trying not to laugh.

'I am wearing them to protect my feet,' said the eldest brother. 'I am terrified of spiders and I shouldn't like one to run across my feet. I think I will be safe in these boots.'

The wicked goblin laughed (it was more of a nasty cackle really) and immediately changed himself into a big spider. He ran towards the eldest brother's feet and was so busy trying to frighten him that he did not notice the smile on the man's face. You see, the eldest brother wasn't afraid of spiders at all. When the spider was near enough he jumped on him with the big boots and killed him.

Of course with the goblin's death, the spell was lifted from the wood. The birds returned, flowers began to grow and the sun shone through the trees. Children gathered bluebells again and the village folk were once more able to take a short cut through the wood on their way to market.

THE SOLDIER DOLL

Every year the Princess Lana shared her birthday with her loyal and devoted subjects. One year she commanded the Royal Band to play all day in the market square, and the next year she sent her Royal Gardeners to plant a rose bush in every garden.

The time came for her eleventh birthday. This was to be the year of her betrothal, and it should have been a time for great rejoicing, but it wasn't. The trouble was that the King had arranged for his daughter to marry a very cold and haughty young Prince (who was, however, very rich) and the Princess didn't fancy him at all. But in spite of her private sorrow the Princess remembered her loyal and devoted subjects and sent her pages to give a toy to every child. All the girls had dolls. All the boys had hoops. The Princess stood at the window and smiled as she heard their delighted cries as they received their gifts and began to play.

That afternoon, while the preparations for her party were in progress, she slipped out into the palace garden to be alone with her thoughts. Suddenly she was startled by a shrill voice and an old woman appeared from the shadow of a large oak tree.

'And what of you, my pretty one?' said the old woman. 'Are you not to have a doll then, and you the birthday girl herself?' And she laughed shrilly.

Nervously the Princess stepped back, for the old woman was very ugly and dirty and the Princess had never met anyone like her before.

'See, I have a gift for you,' the old woman continued, and she thrust a small grimy bundle into the Princess's hands. 'Care for it always and it will bring you your heart's desire!'

Remembering her manners the Princess began to

stammer her thanks, but the old woman disappeared as suddenly as she had come. Quickly she unwrapped the bundle and was dismayed to find a small soldier doll, roughly carved from a piece of wood. The uniform was faded and the painted face chipped and worn.

'Well, you're a sad little doll and no mistake,' she

said. 'But you are not to blame for your condition. I will treasure you as I treasure all my birthday gifts and you will bring me my heart's desire. . . . But what *is* my heart's desire, I wonder?'

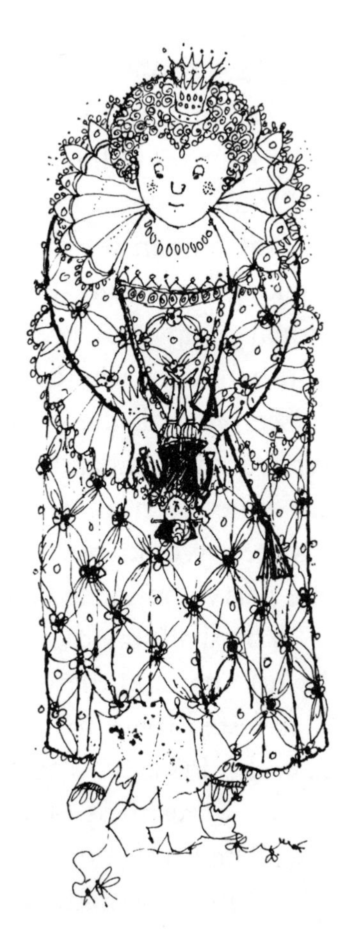

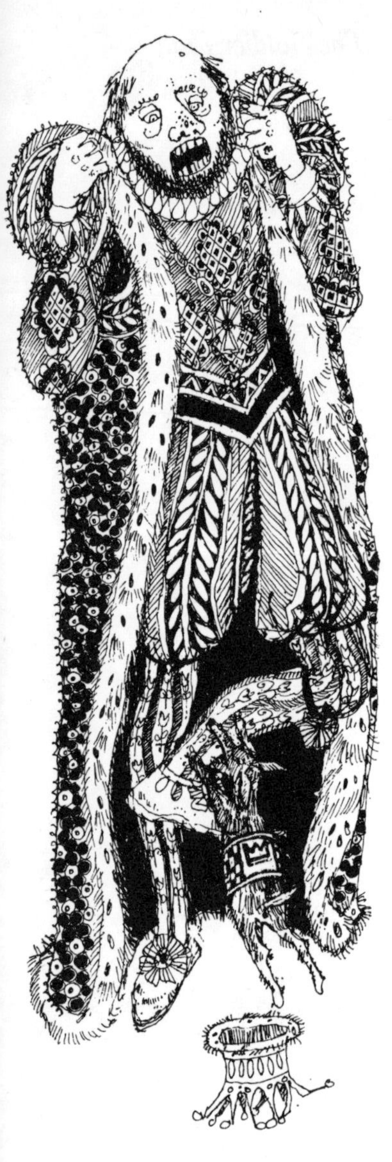

As she made her way back to the palace she thought deeply – and suddenly she knew that what she most desired was to be free of the cold and haughty Prince! She marched straight to her father and said, 'Father, I do not love the cold and haughty Prince you have chosen for me. I do not wish to marry him.'

The King nearly had a fit! It was quite unheard of for a Princess to have any views on such a matter. He fell into a terrible rage. He shouted and roared until he was blue in the face and he stamped his foot. He took off his crown and threw it on to the ground. He stormed up and down the room waving his arms and he kicked the Royal Dog who came running in to see what all the noise was about. The Royal Dog was very put out and bit the King's ankle which made his rage even more terrible. Finally, because the Princess would not change her mind, he cancelled the party and locked her in her room.

'You shall stay there until you change your mind!' he told her and there the matter rested.

It rested there for a very long time. Years passed and the Princess would not change her mind. The Prince grew tired of waiting and married someone else. The loyal and devoted subjects began to worry. The Princess would soon be fifteen years old and that was the age for Royal Princesses to be married. They did not want her to marry the wrong man, but on the other hand not to be married at all would be a great disgrace for the entire kingdom. It was a very difficult time for everyone.

Princess Lana, meanwhile, had grown from a happy, lively girl into a sad and lonely young woman. She had no one to talk to except the little soldier doll and he was her only comfort. Without him her life would have been wretched indeed.

One day the King called all his people together and made the following announcement.

'The Princess Lana is this day formally betrothed to King Boris of Uphalia. The wedding will take place one month from today.'

There was a great uproar at his words and the Princess began to weep bitterly. King Boris was a very old, fat, greedy, selfish, boring man and the Princess didn't fancy him, either, but the King told her he would put up with no more of her nonsense.

'Two guards will escort you to the church,' he said, 'and there will be no running away. My present to you will be a solid gold toast rack.'

The day of the wedding arrived and it seemed that there was no hope for the poor Princess. Sadly she

put on her wedding gown (which was of white lace with silver ribbon round the hem and small silver roses scattered over the bodice) and picked up the little soldier doll.

'You have comforted me for many years,' she said. 'I cannot be without you today.'

The guards arrived and led her through the streets which were full of silent people. There were no cheers, but a few boos for the guards who looked very embarrassed but were, after all, only doing their job. At last the Princess stood beside King Boris and it was at that moment that a very old, very ugly woman pushed her way to stand before them.

'Show me the doll, Princess,' she commanded, and the young bride-to-be held out the soldier doll. The old woman touched it lightly and it was immediately changed into a real soldier. She, too, was changed – from an old woman into a beautiful fairy god-mother with a fairy wand. The Princess stared at the soldier and he smiled.

'I have no riches to offer you,' he said, 'but a loving heart. Will you come with me to be *my* bride?'

Of course, no girl in her right mind would refuse such an offer, and in less time than it takes to tell, the fairy god-mother waved her wand and a white horse appeared. The soldier sprang up on to its back and helped the Princess Lana to do the same and, before the King could collect his wits, they had gone.

No one ever doubted that they lived happily ever after, but we can never be sure. You see, they were never seen again.

THE REALLY DREADFUL DRAGON

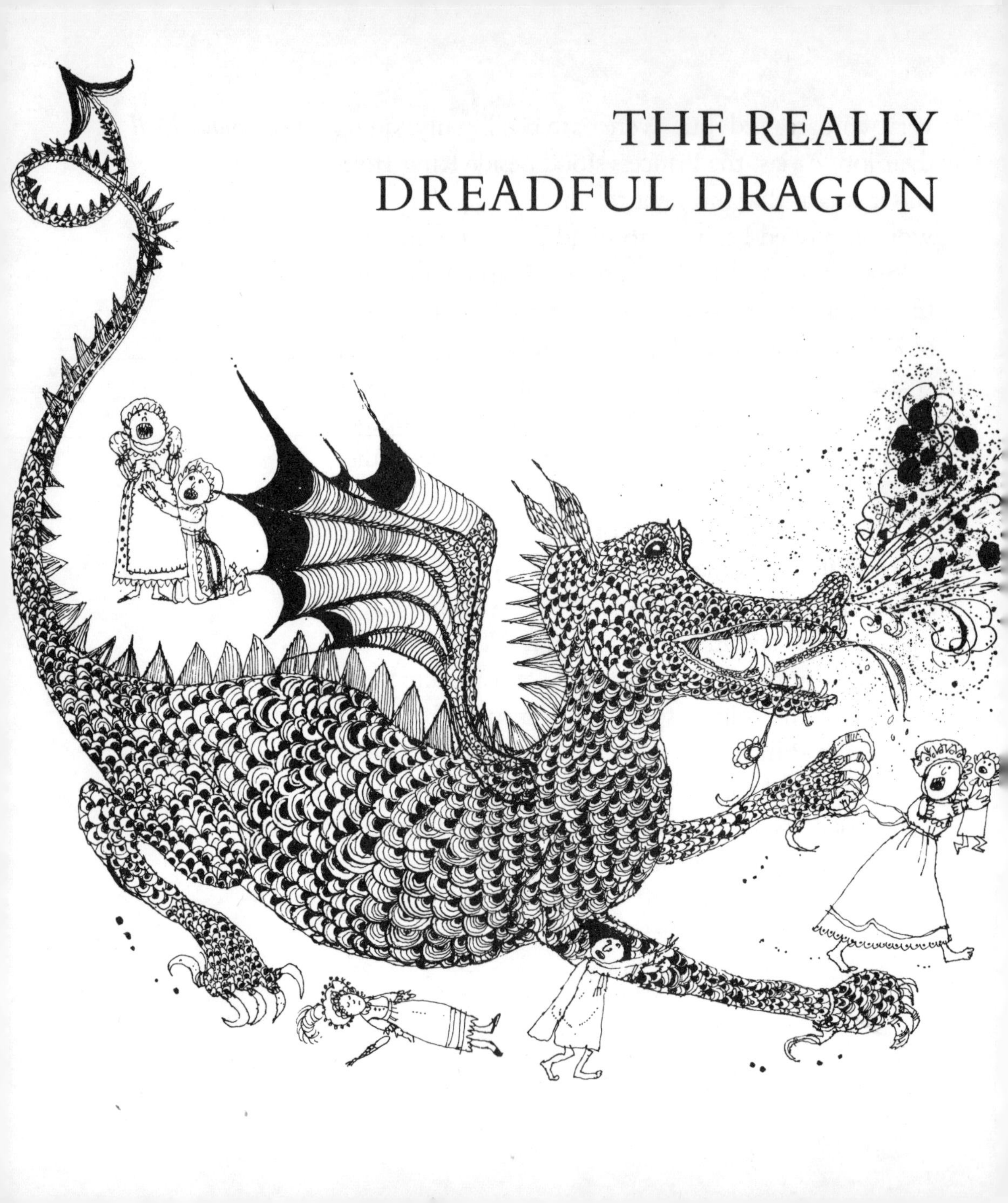

The Really Dreadful Dragon

This story about the dragon is rather bloodthirsty so if you don't like bloodthirsty stories you'd better not read it . . .

When I say dreadful I mean dreadful. The dragon lived in a cave just outside a small town and he terrorised the townsfolk from morning till night. At regular intervals he would descend on the town, breathing smoke and flames and roaring and lashing his long spiked tail and flapping his big green leather wings. He would set fire to a cottage or two and would then seize two or three children and gobble them up. (I told you it was going to be bloodthirsty!)

Occasionally a very brave man would set out to slay the dragon but none had succeeded. Always the dragon, who slept with one eye open, would see the glint of sunlight on the man's sword. One puff from his flaming nostrils would burn the poor fellow to a crisp and his brave sword would be no more than a few drops of molten metal on the ground.

In desperation the Mayor offered one hundred pieces of gold to anyone who could rid the town of the dragon but no one dared. The golden pieces lay for many years unclaimed in a small cloth bag in the Mayor's parlour.

Now at about this time a young soldier returned

from the wars and he chanced one day upon an old woman at a well. She was struggling to wind up the bucket and gallantly he offered to help her for he was a kindly soul. The handle was rusty and the bucket heavy but at last it drew level with the top of the well. The soldier was surprised to see that it contained not water, but a frothy blue liquid which bubbled and spat.

The old woman lifted the bucket from its hook and stood it on the ground. Reaching forward she took the sword from the young soldier and dipped it into the strange liquid. Then she held it aloft so that the blue drops ran down and covered the entire blade.

'Now take it,' commanded the witch (I expect you had guessed), 'and trust it with your life. It will not fail you.' So saying she disappeared. The soldier went on his way, pondering the strange event, and little realising how soon he would be putting her words to the test.

Before noon he came to the town where the really dreadful dragon had just eaten a horse and burnt down the Mayor's house. As soon as the people saw that he was a soldier they fell on their knees and begged him to rid them of the dragon. They told him of the hundred pieces of gold which had just been rescued from the fire. Now although he was a brave young man, a dragon was something he had not bargained for, but he agreed to try. He set off towards the dragon's cave with the cheers of the townsfolk ringing in his ears.

The dragon was lying outside his cave in the sunshine, fast asleep, with one eye open to catch the glint of sunlight on any approaching sword. But on this occasion he did not see a glint of sunlight. He did

not even see a sword, for, unknown to the soldier, the old witch's magic had made the blade invisible to dragons. The dragon thought that the fellow approaching was unarmed and promptly returned to his dragon dreams. The soldier strode bravely forward and plunged his sword deep into the dragon's heart.

It was such a shock for the dragon that he developed a nasty attack of hiccups. Hiccups is no joke if you are in the habit of breathing out smoke and fire and suddenly start breathing them in. Within seconds the dragon burst into flames and was soon burnt to a very large crisp, and the young soldier was the hero of the hour.

The town gave a great banquet in his honour. They had ham and cress rolls, and cheese and cucumber sandwiches (cut into triangles and with the crusts cut off) and sausages (those little ones on sticks) and a cheese dip with cream crackers, and celery, and mushroom vol-au-vents and fruit salad and cream, and chocolate éclairs and pink and white meringues and cheesecake and sherry trifle and ice cream and lemonade and Coca-Cola and cider (for the grown-ups). You can see that as banquets go it was quite something.

They wanted the young soldier to settle in the town but he was homesick. With his trusty sword by his side, and the bag of golden pieces clutched firmly in his hand, he went happily on his way.

THE GOLDEN PRINCESS

Most fairy-tale princesses have golden curls and big blue eyes and this one was no exception. She also had a loving heart and everyone in the kingdom loved her and they called her their golden princess. Now most fairy-tale kings are noble and well intentioned but this one was not. He was as dark as his daughter was fair, and he had a heart to match. He was cold and selfish and the people hated him. They longed for the day when his daughter would reign in his place, for he had no sons to succeed him.

As the years went by the King grew very jealous of his daughter and he made up his mind to get rid of her. He soon discovered, however, that it was not as easy as he expected. He took her into a very dark wood and left her there, but a princess is not the sort of thing you can leave around and hope no one will notice. A kindly woodcutter found her and took her home to the palace where he was rewarded with a bag of gold from the Queen. Next day the King gave the Princess a poisoned cake for her tea, but being a generous soul she gave it to his favourite wolf-hound who gobbled it hungrily. He then rolled slowly on to his back with his legs in the air and was suddenly quite dead.

But the King was a very determined man. A week later he hired an unkempt ruffian to kill the Golden Princess and, at last, everything seemed to be going his way. The unkempt ruffian hid behind a boulder and waited for the Princess to pass on her afternoon

ride, but her horse lost a shoe or something, and there was a long delay. When she finally rode past the boulder the poor man had been crouching there for so long that he had terrible cramp in his legs. When he tried to jump out on her, he fell and stabbed himself in the knee.

The sight of so much blood made him feel quite faint and it was lucky for him that the Golden Princess just happened to have a burnt feather with her. She waved it under his nose and revived him and he went home a changed man. He gave up being an unkempt ruffian and took a job as an assistant librarian . . . but that's another story.

The poor King was getting desperate, and at last he took the Golden Princess for a long walk to the top of a cliff and pushed her over. Of course, she wasn't killed because fairy-tale princesses never are. She fell into a little tree half way down and it took her a long time to climb up the cliff again. By the time she reached the top it was dark. She wandered around feeling very miserable until she saw the lights of a little cottage. Thankfully she ran and knocked on the door, but it simply wasn't her day. The cottage was the home of a wicked old witch who instantly turned the Princess into stone and placed her in the garden among the many other statues of people who had stumbled into her clutches.

The King returned to the palace with a heart-rending account of how his daughter had insisted on going too near to the edge of the cliff and had fallen to certain death amid the waves and rocks below. He went into mourning of darkest black (which he fancied suited him rather well), and the whole kingdom was plunged into an agony of grief and despair. Years passed and more years until the King eventually took sick and died of a rather nasty fever (but hardly anybody missed him). Soon after that the wicked old witch died of old age, and the Queen died of a broken heart. The kingdom was in a very sorry state with no one to rule over it.

One day a handsome Prince came riding by on his snow white horse and as he passed the old witch's cottage his horse stumbled and fell, throwing him to the ground. As he was about to re-mount he noticed the many statues in the cottage garden. Clearing a path through the tangle of weeds and grasses he found himself looking at a statue of a young girl. He instantly recognised the Golden Princess, who had fallen to her death so many years before. The sight filled him with pity for the warm heart now so cold and grey and he gently stroked the stone curls and wept. As his tears fell on to the statue he suddenly felt the curls soften beneath his fingers and the cold stone grew warm. The spell was broken by his tears and the Golden Princess stood before him, shading her eyes from the bright sunlight.

You can imagine the rest of the story for yourself – the wonderful homecoming and the great rejoicing. Of course, the Golden Princess and the handsome Prince were soon married and their two kingdoms became one, and long and wisely did they rule.